2005 HOT POP SINGLES

Arranged by DAN COATES

Remember When It Rained
JOSH GROBAN

STAR WARS (MAIN TITLE)
(From Star Wars®: Episode III Revenge of the Sith)
Music by JOHN WILLIAMS

BOULEVARD OF BROKEN DREAMS
Recorded by
GREEN DAY
Words by BILLIE JOE
Music by GREEN DAY

INSIDE YOUR HEAVEN
Recorded by CARRIE UNDERWOOD on RCA Records
Words and Music by ANDREAS CARLSSON, PER NYLEN and SAVAN KOTECHA

AMERICA'S AVIATION HERO
(from THE AVIATOR)
Composed by HOWARD SHORE

THE AVIATOR

Welcome to My Life
Recorded by SIMPLE PLAN
Words and Music by SIMPLE PLAN

SIMPLE PLAN

JOHN TRAVOLTA
From Be Cool
UMA THURMAN
BELIEVER
Recorded by CHRISTINA MILIAN on TVT Records
Words and Music by will.i.am and John Legend

Dan Coates

As a student at the University of Miami, Dan Coates paid his tuition by playing the piano at south Florida nightclubs and restaurants. One evening in 1975, after Dan had worked his unique brand of magic on the ivories, a stranger from the music field walked up and told him that he should put his inspired piano arrangements down on paper so they could be published.

Dan took the stranger's advice—and the world of music has become much richer as a result. Since that chance encounter long ago, Dan has gone on to achieve international acclaim for his brilliant piano arrangements. His *Big Note, Easy Piano* and *Professional Touch* arrangements have inspired countless piano students and established themselves as classics against which all other works must be measured.

Enjoying an exclusive association with Warner Bros. Publications since 1982, Dan has demonstrated a unique gift for writing arrangements intended for students of every level, from beginner to advanced. Dan never fails to bring a fresh and original approach to his work. Pushing his own creative boundaries with each new manuscript, he writes material that is musically exciting and educationally sound.

From the very beginning of his musical life, Dan has always been eager to seek new challenges. As a five-year-old in Syracuse, New York, he used to sneak into the home of his neighbors to play their piano. Blessed with an amazing ear for music, Dan was able to imitate the melodies of songs he had heard on the radio. Finally, his neighbors convinced his parents to buy Dan his own piano. At that point, there was no stopping his musical development. Dan won a prestigious New York State competition for music composers at the age of 15. Then, after graduating from high school, he toured the world as an arranger and pianist with the group Up With People.

Later, Dan studied piano at the University of Miami with the legendary Ivan Davis, developing his natural abilities to stylize music on the keyboard. Continuing to perform professionally during and after his college years, Dan has played the piano on national television and at the 1984 Summer Olympics in Los Angeles. He has also accompanied recording artists as diverse as Dusty Springfield and Charlotte Rae.

During his long and prolific association with Warner Bros. Publications, Dan has written many award-winning books. He conducts piano workshops worldwide, demonstrating his famous arrangements with a special spark that never fails to inspire students and teachers alike.

BIO01 2/23/04

CONTENTS

BREAKAWAY

Words and Music by
MATTHEW GERRARD, AVRIL LAVIGNE
and BRIDGET BENENATE
Arranged by DAN COATES

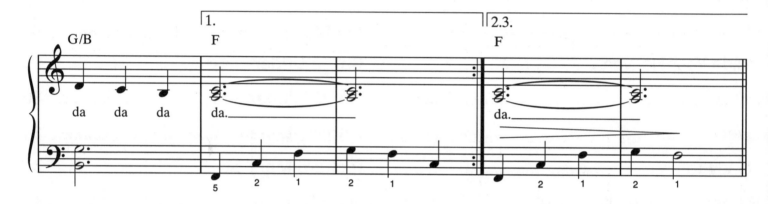

Verse:

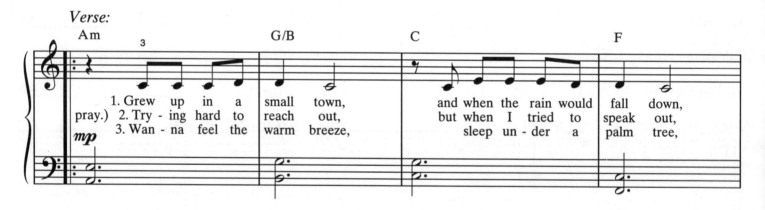

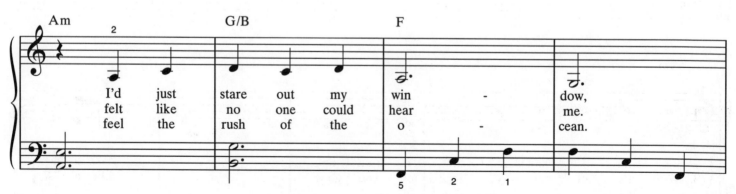

Breakaway - 4 - 1

BOULEVARD OF BROKEN DREAMS

Words by BILLIE JOE
Music by GREEN DAY
Arranged by DAN COATES

Verses 1 & 2:

1. I walk a lone-ly road, the on-ly one that I have ev-er
2. I'm walk-ing down the line that di-vides me some-where in my

known. Don't know where it goes, but it's home to me and I walk a-
mind. On the bor-der-line of the edge and where I walk a-

lone.
lone.
    I walk this emp-ty street
    Read be-tween the lines of

Boulevard of Broken Dreams - 4 - 1

10

AMERICA'S AVIATION HERO
(from THE AVIATOR)

Composed by
HOWARD SHORE
Arranged by DAN COATES

BELIEVER

Words and Music by
will.i.am and John Legend
Arranged by DAN COATES

Slowly and freely

Verse:

(l.h. simile)

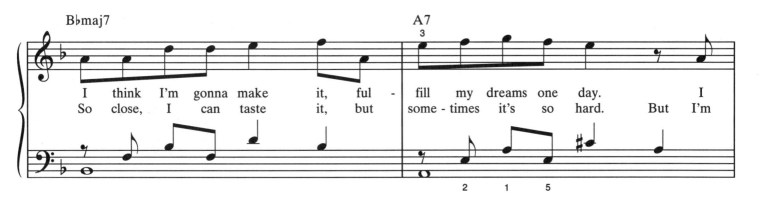

1. Life is what you make it. At least, that's what they say. Well, I think I'm gonna make it, ful - fill my dreams one day. I

2. Ev - 'ry day I'm wait - ing, trying to find my pa - tience. So close, I can taste it, but some - times it's so hard. But I'm

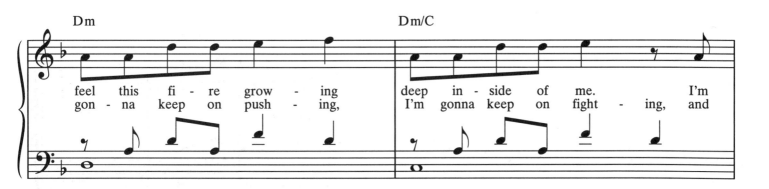

feel this fi - re grow - ing deep in - side of me. I'm

gon - na keep on push - ing, I'm gonna keep on fight - ing, and

Believer - 3 - 1

16

Chorus:

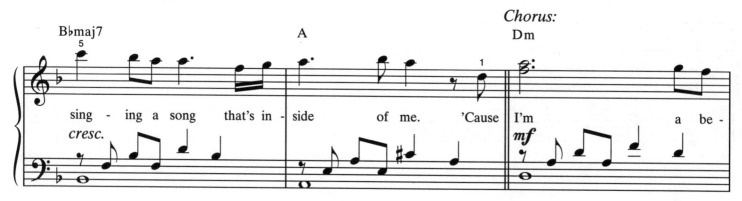

Believer - 3 - 2

EMOTIONAL

Words and Music by
ANDREAS CARLSSON,
DESMOND CHILD and CHRIS BRAIDE
Arranged by DAN COATES

Emotional - 4 - 1

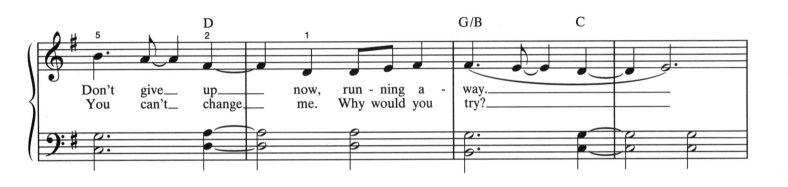

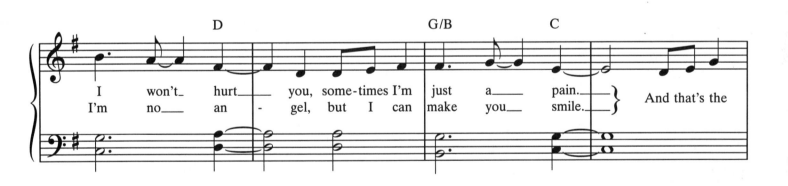

FLY

Words and Music by
JOHN SHANKS and KARA DIOGUARDI
Arranged by DAN COATES

Moderately slow

Verses 1 & 2:

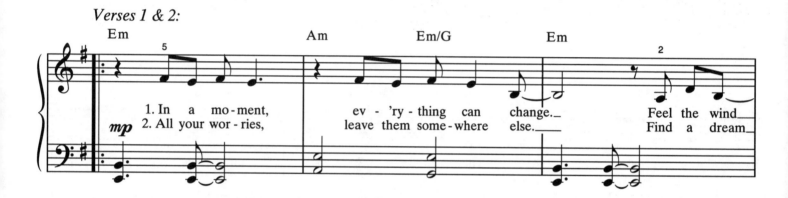

1. In a mo-ment, ev-'ry-thing can change.__ Feel the wind__
2. All your wor-ries, leave them some-where else.__ Find a dream__

__ on your shoul-der. For a min-ute, all the world can wait.__
__ you can fol-low. Reach for some-thing when there's noth-ing left__

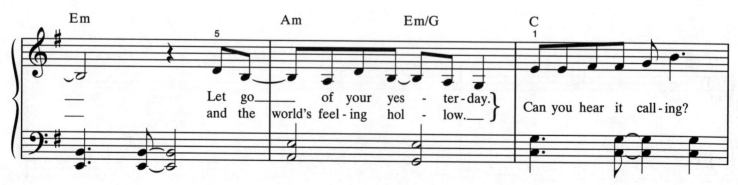

Let go__ of your yes-ter-day.} Can you hear it call-ing?
and the world's feel-ing hol-low.__

Fly - 4 - 1

24

INSIDE YOUR HEAVEN

Words and Music by
ANDREAS CARLSSON, PER NYLEN
and SAVAN KOTECHA
Arranged by DAN COATES

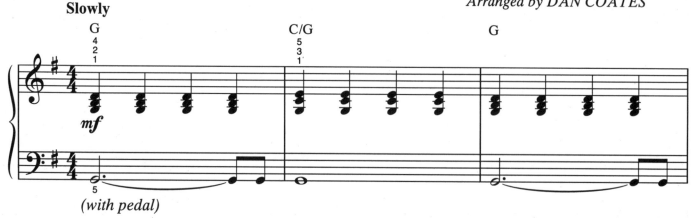

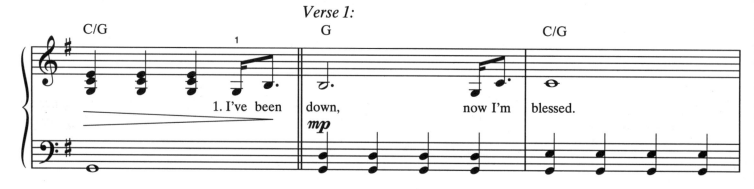

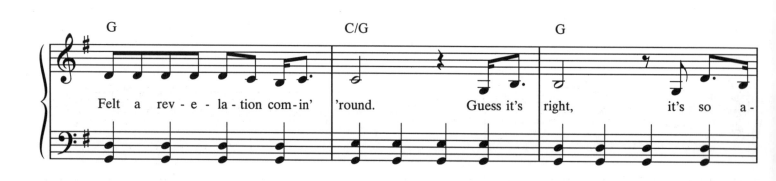

Inside Your Heaven - 4 - 1

28

MY LOVE IS HERE

Words and Music by
JIM BRICKMAN, DAVID GROW
and ROCH VOISINE
Arranged by DAN COATES

My Love Is Here - 4 - 1

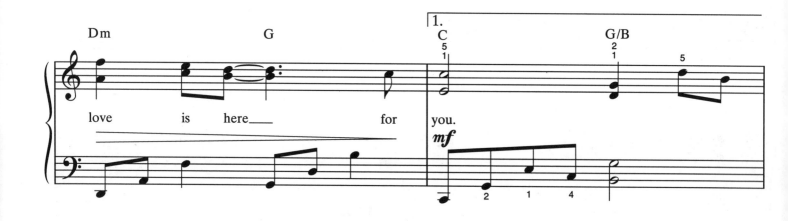

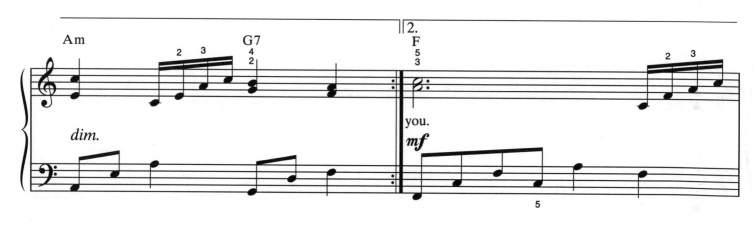

OVER

Words and Music by
JOHN SHANKS, KARA DIOGUARDI
and LINDSAY LOHAN
Arranged by DAN COATES

Over - 5 - 1

38

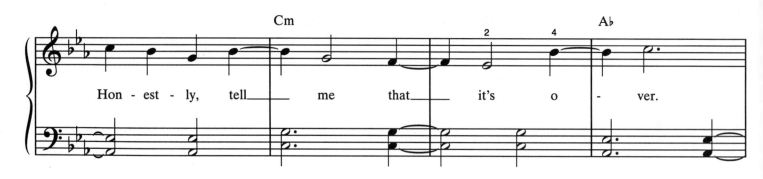

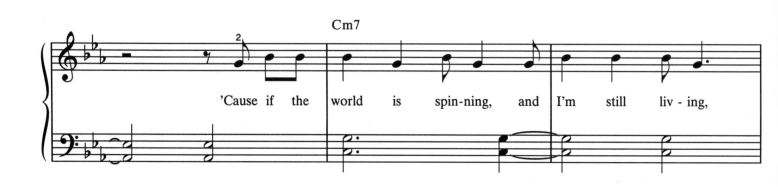

Over - 5 - 5

READY TO FLY

Words and Music by
RICHARD MARX
Arranged by DAN COATES

Slowly (♩. = 44)

Verse:

1. I've been try-ing to o-pen the door to the
2. Rest-less, hope-less and mis-un-der-stood, like

se-cret of my des-ti-ny. And
so man-y oth-ers I know.

ev-er-y new road I think is the one____
So bus-y try-ing to keep hold-ing on,____ when

seems to lead right back to me.____ I've
I should have been let-ting go.____ I've been

looked for a way to be wis-er, a way to be
giv-en the gift of all of my find-ing the spi-rit be in my
an-swer to won-der is right in my

Ready to Fly - 5 - 1

42

REMEMBER WHEN IT RAINED

Lyrics by
JOSH GROBAN

Music by ERIC MOUQUET
and JOSH GROBAN
Arranged by DAN COATES

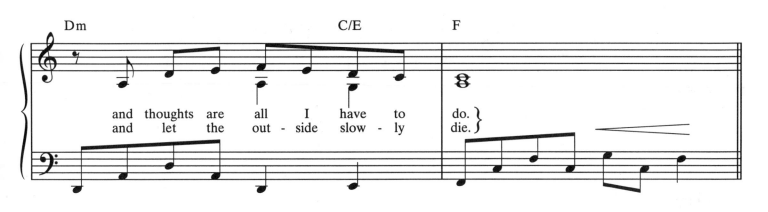

Chorus:

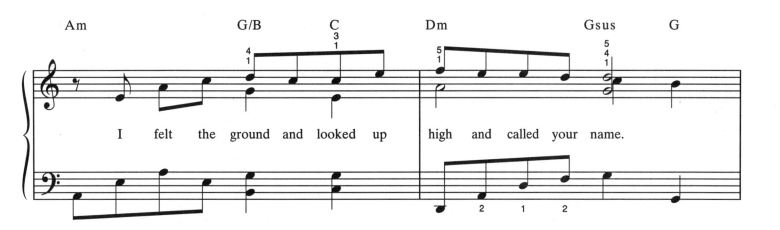

In the dark - ness I re - main._____

dim.

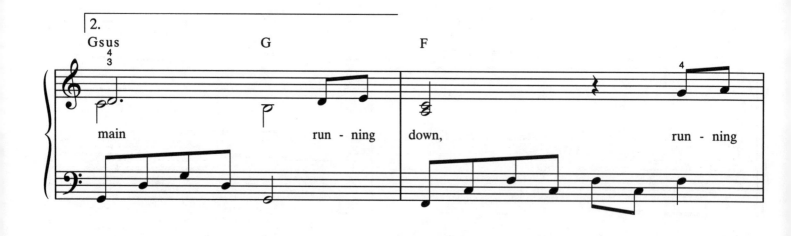

main   run - ning   down,   run - ning

down,   run - ning   down,   run - ning

48

WELCOME TO MY LIFE

Words and Music by
SIMPLE PLAN
Arranged by DAN COATES

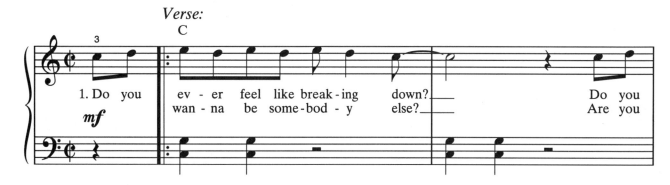

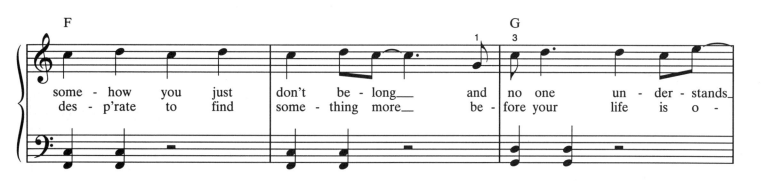

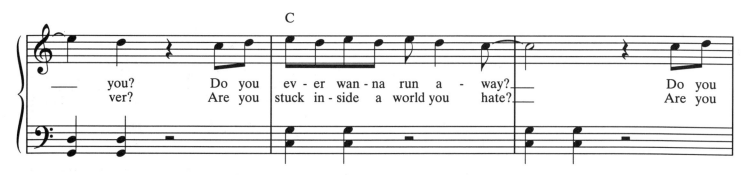

Welcome to My Life - 5 - 1

50

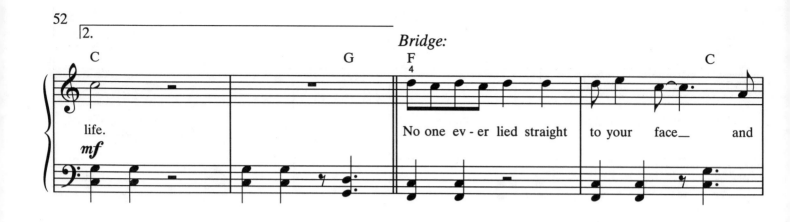

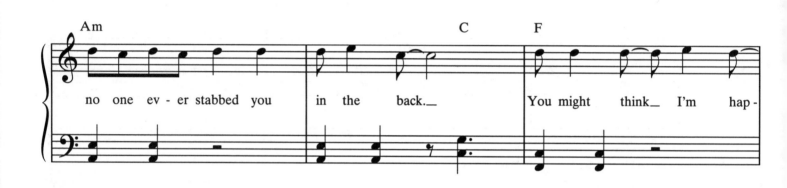

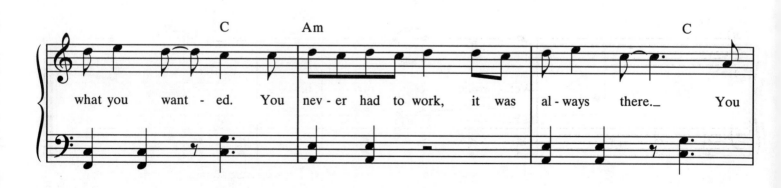

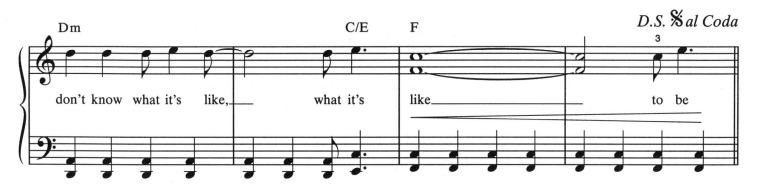

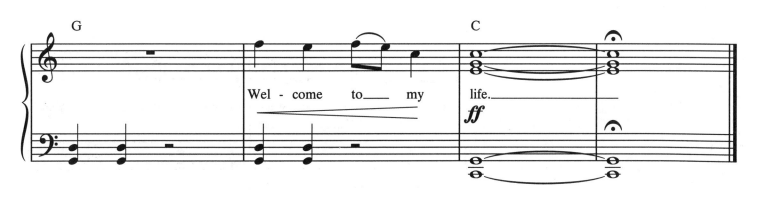

From the Twentieth Century-Fox Motion Picture "STAR WARS"

STAR WARS
(Main Title)

Music by
JOHN WILLIAMS
Arranged by DAN COATES

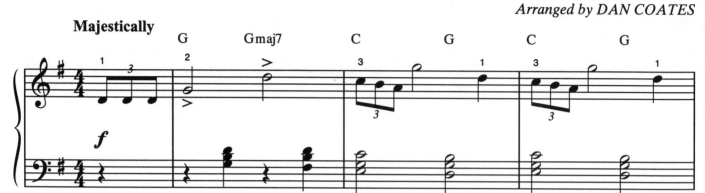

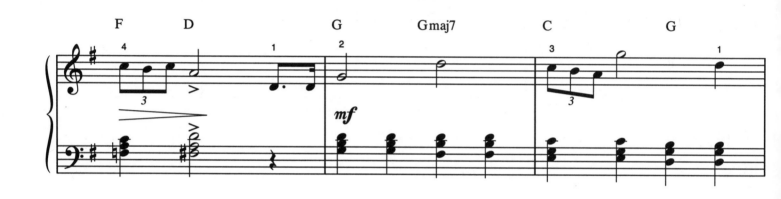

Star Wars - 2 - 1

UNTITLED
(How Could This Happen to Me?)

Words and Music by
SIMPLE PLAN
Arranged by DAN COATES

Untitled (How Could This Happen to Me?) - 4 - 1

58

WHEN YOU TELL ME THAT YOU LOVE ME

Words and Music by
ALBERT HAMMOND and JOHN BETTIS
Arranged by DAN COATES

When You Tell Me That You Love Me - 5 - 1

When You Tell Me That You Love Me - 5 - 4

64

shin - ing like a can - dle in the dark when you tell me that you

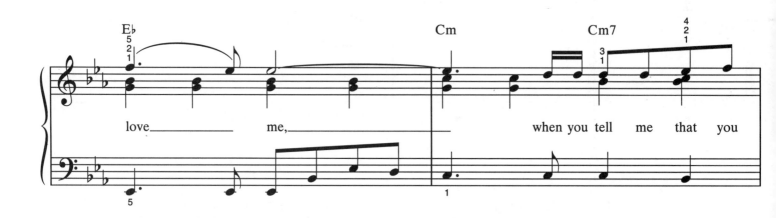

love _____ me, _____ when you tell me that you

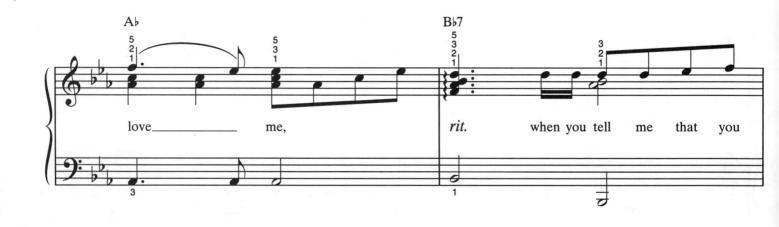

love _____ me, *rit.* when you tell me that you

love me.